21st
Century
Skills Library

ROAD TO RECOVERY
KEY DEER

Susan H. Gray

Cherry Lake Publishing
Ann Arbor, Michigan

Published in the United States of America by Cherry Lake Publishing
Ann Arbor, MI
www.cherrylakepublishing.com

Content Adviser: Professor Roel R. Lopez, Department of Wildlife and Fisheries Sciences, Texas A&M University, College Station, Texas

Photo Credits: Pages 4 and 26, Photo courtesy of U.S. Fish and Wildlife Service; pages 5, 19, and 24, Photo courtesy of Lana Law; pages 6, 11, 12, 16, 20, 22, and 28, Photo courtesy of Ken Araujo, www.kenaraujo.com; page 7, © Buddy Mays/Corbis; page 10, Photo courtesy of Marv Dembinsky, www.dpaphoto.com; page 14, Photo courtesy of Mark Averette

Map by XNR Productions Inc.

Library of Congress Cataloging-in-Publication Data
Gray, Susan Heinrichs.
 Key deer / by Susan H. Gray.
    p. cm. — (Road to recovery)
 ISBN-13: 978-1-60279-039-1 (hardcover)
 ISBN-10: 1-60279-039-6 (hardcover)
 1. White-tailed deer. I. Title. II. Series.
 QL737.U55G73 2007
 599.65'2—dc22   2007004219

*Cherry Lake Publishing would like to acknowledge the work of
The Partnership for 21st Century Skills.
Please visit* www.21stcenturyskills.org *for more information.*

TABLE OF CONTENTS

CHAPTER ONE

An Evening Snack

A Key deer and her baby feed on plants on the Florida Keys.

The sun is setting, and the air is beginning to cool. Dusk is settling over

Florida, and the Key deer are becoming active. A mother deer leads her

baby to a clump of tree cactus. The plants are covered with sharp spines.

Key deer live only on the Florida Keys.

A **species** is a group of similar animals or plants. Grizzly bears, blue jays, and great white sharks are examples of species. Some species have members that live in their own areas, away from the others. Often, they will adapt and change to fit their new environment. These separate groups are called **subspecies**. The Key deer is a subspecies of the Virginia white-tailed deer. What kind of environmental differences do you think would cause a subspecies to develop?

But here and there are flowers and juicy red fruits.

Mother and baby nibble at the fruits, careful to avoid the stinging spines. After a few minutes, they finish their snack and move on.

Key deer spend most of their days searching for food.

CHAPTER TWO

LIFE OF THE KEY DEER

Coral flats are visible just under the surface of the water in this aerial view of the Florida Keys. The Keys are part of one of the world's largest coral reef ecosystems.

Key deer live only on the Florida Keys. The Keys are a chain of U.S. islands off the southern tip of Florida. The chain is about 128 miles (206 kilometers) long.

The area's Key deer are small animals, about 30 inches (76 centimeters) tall at the shoulder. Females are called **does**, and males are called **bucks**. As adults, does weigh up to 65 pounds (29 kilograms) and bucks weigh up to 80 pounds (36 kg).

Key deer feed on a wide variety of plants. Their favorite is the mangrove.

These animals have tan, reddish, or gray coats. Their chests and bellies are white. Many deer also have a dark Y-shaped marking on the face.

There are hundreds of islands in the Keys, but most Key deer live on two of them—Big Pine Key and No Name Key. The rest of the deer live on about 20 other nearby Keys, where they have plenty of food and freshwater. The deer cannot drink salty ocean water. So they live on islands where ponds fill with rainwater.

The deer feed on more than 160 kinds of plants. One of their favorite foods is the **mangrove**. Mangroves are trees and shrubs that live in moist, swampy areas. They are plentiful on the Florida Keys.

Key deer seem to have favorite places on the islands. They travel the same trails over and over. They visit the same areas to feed and sleep. And they often go to the same spots along roadways in order to cross.

In the fall, bucks begin looking for mates. They compete with each other by butting heads. Sometimes this contest ends in injury for the loser and a doe for the winner.

Baby Key deer, or fawns, weigh only a few pounds at birth. In their first few weeks, they gain weight quickly and grow rapidly.

Baby deer, or fawns, are born from April through June. They weigh between 2 and 4 pounds (0.9 and 1.8 kg). The fawns have long, **spindly** legs and big ears. Their reddish brown coats are dotted with white.

21st CENTURY SKILLS LIBRARY

The Keys get the most rainfall in the spring and summer months.

Ponds on the islands fill up, and plants sprout new leaves. Then the does

and their fawns have plenty of food and freshwater.

The deer also know how to cope during dry months. If water dries

up on one Key, they swim to another nearby island. Most Keys are between

1 and 4 miles (1.6 and 6.4 km) apart, but some are much closer.

Key Deer can easily swim between the Keys.

Learning & Innovation Skills

The Key deer are members of a family of animals called cervids. This family also includes moose, elk, and reindeer. Cervids are plant eaters, dining on moss, grass, and leaves. They have slender legs and tough hooves. Most cervids have coats that are gray, brown, or reddish brown. As babies, their coats are spotted with white. Can you name any other members of the cervid family?

Male Key deer grow antlers in the spring and shed them in the winter.

12

As males get older, they begin to grow antlers. This growth starts in the late spring. The developing antlers are covered with soft fuzz called velvet. Velvet is actually a layer of skin that contains blood vessels. In the fall, bucks kick or scrape off their velvet. This does not hurt the animals. But it might make their antlers look ragged or shaggy. In the winter, their antlers fall off completely. Then spring comes, and they start to grow new ones.

Female Key deer live longer than males. Does usually live about six or seven years, while bucks live to be about three or four.

21st Century Content

The Key deer is a dwarf version of the American white-tailed deer. It weighs between 45 and 80 pounds (20 and 36 kg). Although the Key deer is small, it is not the smallest deer in the world. The smallest deer is the pudú, which weighs between 20 and 33 pounds (9 and 15 kg) and is about 15 inches (38 cm) tall. Pudús live in the Andes mountain range along the western coast of South America.

CHAPTER THREE

KEY DEER IN TROUBLE

*As towns and cities grew on the Florida Keys, it
became harder for the Key deer to find food.*

Scientists believe the Key deer have lived on Florida's Keys for thousands

of years. They certainly were there in the 1500s when a Spanish shipwreck

A Key deer walks with her fawn near a developed area.
Key deer have become accustomed to seeing humans.

Germs were yet another threat. Bucks were passing a brain infection to each other. The animals shared germs when they butted heads during the breeding season. The infection did not kill the deer but made the animals unsteady and dizzy. The deer wandered onto dangerous roads or fell into ponds and drowned.

There was one other problem. Most does give birth to only one baby each year. But every year, more deer died from natural and unnatural causes than

Learning & Innovation Skills

Key deer, like other plant eaters, help to spread plant seeds. The deer eat fruit and berries in addition to leaves and grass. The fruit and berries contain seeds that end up in the deer's droppings. As the deer move about, the plant seeds are scattered far and wide.

By eating one fruit in particular, the Key deer are actually helping another **endangered** species. The Key tree cactus nearly became **extinct** a century ago and is still endangered today. It is a tall, slender cactus that needs shade to survive. It lives in only one place in the world—the Florida Keys.

The tree cactus produces a bright-red fruit. Birds and other animals, including the Key deer, nibble on the fruit, then spread the seeds everywhere. It is helping the tree cactus to survive. It is an unusual case of one endangered species aiding another. Can you think of any other animals that help a plant survive?

were born. The births were not keeping up with the

deaths. So year after year, the deer numbers shrank.

By 1950, there were probably fewer than 50 Key deer

left on Earth.

In 1967, the U.S. government said the Key deer

was an endangered species. This meant that the

deer was close to disappearing completely. Without

a change, the Key deer would soon be lost to the

natural world.

CHAPTER FOUR

THE ROAD TO RECOVERY

*Although Florida state law banned the hunting of Key deer
in 1939, only about 50 animals were left by 1950.*

Peole finally saw that something had to be done to save the Key deer.

Government officials, wildlife workers, and ordinary citizens got busy. In

*This Key deer on Big Pine Key wears a radio collar
so scientists can monitor its activity.*

1957, the government created the National Key Deer **Refuge**. It included

thousands of acres on 25 Keys.

The state and county also set aside land for the deer. Government officials made laws against hunting the deer, feeding them, and speeding on roads they usually crossed. Local officials also began to trap dogs that ran loose. They put limits on where homes could be built.

Scientists and volunteers got involved, too. They began teaching everyone about the deer. They spoke on radio and television about how the deer became endangered. And they explained why it was harmful to feed the deer.

Scientists also studied the habits of the Key deer. They put radio collars on the animals and tracked

Life & Career Skills

In 2006, wildlife workers with the U.S. government worked with local officials on an exciting new plan to protect the Key deer. The plan set aside more land on the Florida Keys for the Key deer. It also limited the number of houses and businesses in the area. These people working together helped to protect not only the Key deer, but other animals as well.

Key deer travel freely between the islands during the wet season,
when fresh drinking water is more readily available.

their movements. When they learned of something harmful to the deer, they looked for solutions.

For example, scientists noticed that many Key deer were dying on two of the refuge islands where many people lived. They realized that more people living on the islands meant more paved roads. And more paved roads meant more cars speeding—and killing Key deer. So the scientists notified law officers and government officials. After that, laws became tougher, and more speeders were caught. New regulations also limited new building projects on the refuge islands. It was all part of the Key deer's road to recovery.

Learning & Innovation Skills

When Big Pine Key became part of the National Key Deer Refuge, about 100 people lived on the island. Today, more than 5,000 people live there! What impact will the increased population have on the Key deer?

CHAPTER FIVE

KEY DEER TODAY

A Key deer nibbles on grass.

Today, there are between 700 and 800 Key deer on the islands. Their

population has increased dramatically in 50 years. However, the deer have

a long way to go.

Key deer remain on the endangered species list because of their low numbers. Fragile populations on individual islands could still easily be wiped out. An outbreak of disease or an environmental change that affects food or water sources could do great damage to the deer population on a single island.

Scientists remain hopeful that the Key deer population can grow in the future.

A Key deer stands in red mangroves in the National Key Deer Refuge, which covers thousands of acres across 25 islands.

Scientists, law officers, and many other people are working to protect

the deer. They are trying to keep the animals in their natural habitat.

Some people are working to make that habitat safer. Others are caring for injured deer until they can be set free.

Some scientists are even moving deer over to other less-**inhabited** islands. These scientists care for the Key deer in pens in their new homes for about six months and then let them loose. This experiment seems to be working. The deer are getting used to the new islands, and their **distribution** is increasing. The scientists hope that one day Key deer will have as much safe habitat as they need.

There will probably never be thousands of Key deer. In fact, there probably never were thousands.

21st Century Content

One of the roles of government is to protect and set aside land for future generations of people and animals to enjoy. The National Key Deer Refuge covers 84,000 acres (33,994 hectares) on the Florida Keys. The refuge is spread over parts of 25 islands and includes forests and **wetlands**. People may visit the refuge, but they are not allowed to feed the deer.

The refuge helps the deer, but it's also good for other living things. Altogether, there are 22 endangered or threatened species of plants and animals there.

In 1989, a group of dedicated citizens got together to found the Key Deer Protection Alliance. Members teach the public about how the Key deer lives and why this animal is important. They also visit schools. These people working together are doing their part to help protect the Key deer.

Most of the Florida Keys are too small to support many deer. But if their numbers keep growing and they are given more safe places to live, the Key deer will no longer be endangered.

Scientists, environmentalists, and animal lovers hope to see the Key deer in safe habitats for years to come.

Florida

Florida Keys

Gulf of Mexico

Lower Florida Keys

Water Keys
Annette Key
Mayo Key
Water Key
Johnson Key
Toptree Hammock Key
Howe Key
Little Pine Key
Knockemdown Key
1
4
Cudjoe Key
3
Big Pine Key
No Name Key
2
Sugarloaf Key
Ramrod Key
Summerland Key
Little Munson Island
Big Munson Island

Key West

ATLANTIC OCEAN

1 Big Torch Key
2 Little Torch Key
3 Middle Torch Key
4 Porpoise Key

0   10 mi
0   10 km

Current range of the Key deer

This map shows where Key deer live in the United States.

GLOSSARY

bucks (BUX) male deer

distribution (diss-tri-BYOO-shuhn) the area over which an animal population normally lives or travels

does (DOHZ) female deer

endangered (en-DAYN-jurd) in danger of dying out completely

extinct (ek-STINGKT) no longer living

inhabited (in-HAB-uh-tid) lived on by people or animals

mangrove (MAN-grove) a type of tree or shrub that grows in warm, wet areas

refuge (REF-yooj) a place of safety and protection

species (SPEE-sheez) a group of similar animals or plants

spindly (SPIND-lee) long and thin

subspecies (SUB-spee-sheez) a smaller group within a species

wetlands (WET-landz) wet, moist lowland areas

FOR MORE INFORMATION

Books

Clark, Margaret Goff. *Save the Florida Key Deer*. New York: Dutton Juvenile, 1998.

Evert, Laura. *Whitetail Deer*. Minnetonka, MN: NorthWord Press, 2000.

Francis, Dorothy Brenner. *Toy Deer of the Florida Keys*.
Logan, IA: Perfection Learning, 2000.

Patent, Dorothy Hinshaw. *Deer and Elk*. New York: Clarion Books, 1994.

Web Sites

Key Deer Protection Alliance
www.keydeer.org
For information about efforts to protect the Key deer

National Key Deer Refuge
www.fws.gov/nationalkeydeer
To read a guide to the National Key Deer Refuge with information about the species

INDEX

ABOUT THE AUTHOR

Susan H. Gray has a master's degree in zoology. She has written more than 70 science and reference books for children and especially loves writing about animals. Gray also likes to garden and play the piano. She lives in Cabot, Arkansas, with her husband, Michael, and many pets.